This Far

POEMS

Kathleen O'Toole

PARACLETE PRESS

BREWSTER, MASSACHUSETTS

Paraclete Poetry Series Editor
Mark S. Burrows

2019 First Printing

This Far: Poems

Copyright © 2019 by Kathleen O'Toole

ISBN 978-1-64060-262-5

The Paraclete Press name and logo (dove on cross) are trademarks of Paraclete Press, Inc.

Library of Congress Control Number:2019945042

10 9 8 7 6 5 4 3 2 1

Published by Paraclete Press
Brewster, Massachusetts
www.paracletepress.com

Printed in the United States of America

CONTENTS

III. What Kind of Silence

NOTES TO THE POEMS
93

ACKNOWLEDGMENTS
95

INTRODUCTION

*having come this far
alive at fifty-five
the morning star*

The convergence of the past with an immediate present and a glimpse of the immanent future, is captured in this haiku by American haiku master Nick Virgilio. His haiku, which inspired the title poem in *This Far*, may well suggest a unifying principle for this collection: the cohabitation, in a moment of heightened attention or artistic creation, of other "time zones" in the life of the artist.

Perhaps music might offer another way of understanding the coherence and architecture of *This Far*. As I gathered these poems—the harvest of one season of life and writing (a decade later than Virgilio's haiku)—they seemed to flow together like linked movements in a musical composition. Thus, I began to think of them as suites of poems whose preoccupations or leitmotifs are related. In one movement: grief and the impulse to honor the "saints" in my personal and creative life. In another: the sacramental power of works of art and the natural world to illuminate life and loss. Finally, poems born of opposing, but not mutually exclusive impulses: the desire to practice monastic silence and contemplation, and the urge to bear witness. I hope that the variety of forms in which these poems arrived, and their shifting elegiac, lyric, or narrative ambitions, are held together by a single voice and consciousness, much as a conductor guides an orchestra.

I trust the reader might find among the natural crescendos of loss and unexpected grace, some familiar chords: a delve into the natural and aesthetic worlds for insight or consolation, an interrogation of inherited truths in the light of crises facing the earth and our human communities, the residue of stories and questions overheard that begged to be transcribed, or further amplified in the telling.

In the end, think of these poems as stones, marking the circuits of one poet's pilgrimage. *This Far*—an offering of solidarity, an invitation to journey.

Mindful

The moment, fleeting as a nuthatch
that alighted on the flowerbox at breakfast,
the lichen-green hummingbird grazing
the impatiens at noon. I toss them
blueberry pits, bread crumbs. This

moment, before a car bomb is planted
beside a schoolyard in Basra,
a swarm of locusts about to alight
on precious maize in Niger. Nuthatch
and nutcracker engineer whole piñón

forests, one seed cache at a time.
The hummingbird's tongue is longer
than its head and beak, longer
than it needs to extract the dusky
pollen at the petunia's throat.

Samsara's in every in-breath, each
shutter click of attention: first warning
signs of famine, children lining up
for the soldiers' candy, wolf lichen
in a gash on the ponderosa's downed limb.

I

Their Voices

Medium

In the valley a red-winged blackbird's call
echoes the keening wind of March. Solo,
atop a utility pole, then a lodgepole pine,
he peddles his sharp, insistent cry. His head
swivels, and I imagine he's following me,
separated from his circle of call and response.
I'm hoping for a medium—four months
and I still can't conjure your voice. The first
weeks after you died, a lone robin visited
my back yard daily. Your grandson found him
oddly friendly, so I would interrogate him:
shape shifter, robbery suspect, your envoy?
You wanted to "go out singing" so why not
return as a robin, the breed your bird-loving
mother Madelyn loved? I loved his singing,
distinct in the dawn chorus, serenading me
at dusk. But even his aria did not unlock
your boisterous baritone from memory. Nor
did you come to me in a dream. So I turned
to beer and baseball, cheered the Phillies' early
season success, watched their sluggers stumble,
even took in the All-Star Game, in your beat-up
recliner no less. No dice; no word.
                                              So I'm back
to birds. I've deciphered a lark's duet
with a twenty-nine-bell carillon in Bruges,
queried a jackdaw on a Brussels balcony,
expecting a message from you. Then today,
the iridescent flash of a stellar's jay
interrupted my lunchtime reverie. He hops,
squawks, and I hear: *What of this beauty*
would I not steal for you—this sky,

the sun, my cobalt brilliance into your joy.
Only that's not your voice, at least not
any voice I'd recognize as yours. Don't
tell me this obsession with song is your gift—
that Jungian saw about receiving your life's
errand from the other-gendered parent. If so,
what did I miss in hearing only the sports
announcer's voice, that voice more rehearsed
for show tunes and audiences (*Something familiar,*
something peculiar, something for everybody . . .)
than for poetry?
              I can still see you
in your last hospital room, my book of poetry
in your hands, curious about the origins,
probing obscurities. You did love the baseball
poem, the one I dedicated to you, but I had to
explain: it was *your* voice I'd channeled.

Reliquary

Bronze and alabaster, filigreed chests and chalices,
boxes and cruciform vessels crafted to contain:
> *the tooth of Mary Magdalen*
> *John the Baptist's jawbone*
> *a thorn from the Crucifixion crown.*

My favorite: carved marble from Syria
enclosing a sliver of St. Baudine's bone, its libation opening
like a tiny Holy Water font, invites the tender to pour
oil or water through the ark, the faithful to anoint
or bless themselves with liquid that has touched
the holy saint's remains.

> I carry my father's First Communion photo
> tied with a blue silk ribbon, in my journal:
> a slight boy in white shorts and stockings, gazing
> at the camera with such intense reverence, rosary beads
> around his folded hands. This, the image we placed
> with a votive candle by the guestbook at his wake.

First, the piety of pilgrims fills the streets of Chartres
to venerate a shred of cloth from Mary's robe, then
a Cathedral to enclose the observance in glorious
stained glass. In Bruges, drops of the Savior's Holy Blood
in rock crystal liquefying at Eastertide for three centuries—
five hundred years congealed, it's still carried in procession
every Trinity Sunday within its own gilded litter.
One saint's relics lodged in a tree in Galway, *can be used to heal*
drunkenness or to protect against nocturnal visits by demons.

As for me, I am unable to discard
the swab we would dip in consecrated wine
to give my father Holy Communion
when he could no longer swallow—the swab
a priest would say we ought to burn. It shall lie
tucked in a drawer, wrapped in cloth
until I bury it under my father's favorite fig tree
in August, or beneath the bird feeder, where
the showers of spent seed with drips of rain
or melting snow will find and encircle it.

Half Italian

The brain's hard-wired with the impulse to feed
when given the chance, and it's why I always double
the garlic in any recipe. The kitchen behind Nonna's
store always smelled of garlic and aged provolone,
but Sundays were drenched with it, especially
right after church. She cooked early and I'd find
any excuse to dig the tin trowel into the sacks
of dried lentils and fagiole, thrilled to feel
them clattering—the clinking of a cartoon king's
gold. Years later I found my way back to the empty
row house, hoping to recover that storefront's hold:
salami-scented floorboards, shelves stocked with tins
of olive oil and anchovies. I only managed to pry
the numbers 4-1-9 from the cracked door frame,
to wrap them in burlap inside her old trunk. Now
nothing renders the essence of Domenica's place
like crushing home-grown basil for pesto Genovese,
pressing garlic into a bowl of extra virgin oil, twice
the measure, plus one clove just for the pleasure.

Terrestrial

Nearly all temperate orchids are terrestrial.
—United States Botanic Garden Orchid Exhibit Guide

I.

Generis Phalaenopsis

She worked her magic
on the Home Depot orchid—
a hasty Mother's Day gift
in a plastic pot—soon its stem
trembled with twenty-eight
purple-lipped blossoms. The cat
couldn't kill it. Nor my father's
errant aim with a fly swatter.
Light, warmth in that picture window—
all important, but it was Mother's
unwavering attention to water,
fertilizer, and rotation that mattered.
She knew nothing special
about orchids, not the difference
between dendrobia and oncidia,
or the standard garden club advice:
repot in small clumps of bark,
rocks, tree fern. These orchids
just like to be rootbound.

II.

Familia Orchidaceae

Cymbidium Merlin, Miltoniopsis
Laelia Sophronitis:
my tongue samples the names
of orchid species on display
in the botanical garden. Just a lunch hour

to savor intoxicating vanilla air,
to let orange-scented vapors
mist my sunglasses. I'm learning
how orchids seduce the birds and insects
they need to pollinate. So Ophrys'
hairy lip conjures the female bee
it must attract; Bulbophyllum
emits the smell of carrion to lure
its fly-partner. Within the sheath
of chemistry's *lingua latina*,
such bonds of fragrant obligation.

III.
Filia Epiphytic

In Maori legend the rainbow shatters
into many shards that lodge in trees
yielding orchids. These epiphytes blossom
roots to air—not parasites,
rather acrobats, who find nourishment
in rainfall, condensation. I discover
their sepals, petals, labella protruding
from rainforest trees, imagine them
breeding with the fungus of high desert
rocks. This extension suits me.
I finally accept our separate ways
of rooting: my orbital impulse,
Mother anchoring in. Time to cut
the stem at an angle, wait
for the stub to fade on its own,
then gather all that's required
for each redolent blossom to unfurl.

Trousseau

A sudden breach of rainwater
into my mother's basement. *First*
time in 63 years. She sends me
to reclaim what can be salvaged.
Half a dozen of my dead father's suits,
a black cocktail dress, size six.
The weathered garment bag
that holds her wedding gown.
I unzip the bag, inside the yellowed satin,
long sleeved for a February wedding.
Its scalloped train looked so glamorous
swirled forward in the studio photos.
Up close, I note it's inexpensive netting,
not lace, so too the veil, stiff and dull,
plucked from its hiding place.
I catch my breath and weigh
my options. For a moment,
I hang it beneath a bare bulb, admire
the modesty of the Peter Pan collar,
above the see-through netting
and tapered satin bodice—touches
she must have chosen.
I bring her the gown, and she explains:
I sketched it out. A little Jewish seamstress
made it for 100 bucks. It would cost
nearly that much to dry clean today.

Sixty-seven years have passed
since it fit her eighteen-inch waist,
its elegance fading through four births,
and all our growing years; six years

since she lost her groom. *Take it away.*
It's making me sad.

To me, then, the task of bagging
the folds of heavy satin into black
plastic for the Tuesday trash. My duty
dispatched, I pause on the porch, where
a late summer breeze stirs memories
of other fabrics: the blue eyelet
of the junior prom gown we sewed
together, that white silk with embossed roses
that she stored in cedar for years, until
I finally wed, scraps of bright floral prints
for quilts we imagined, but never made.
All we've deftly stitched, are stitching still.

From Birdsong

—for my mother

Her fascination with the sparrows at the feeder,
my obsession with birdsong, perhaps a start—
wading into this grief seems like launching
a slight raft out onto a snow-fed creek
the rushing creek that over time will create a canyon.

On a Sierra retreat, I'm enthralled with birds
and birdsong, I learn of avian constraint: birds
the same size, same shape, can only distinguish
themselves with song; of the mountain chickadee
signing threat with the number of notes in her call;
of golden eagles, navigating wind currents by memory.

Today a naturalist spoke of the risk that birds take
just to sing, revealing themselves to predators.
So when you hear a bird sing, *she must have
something important to say*. These days
when my mother speaks of Dad's death, she says:
We thought we had at least another year.

I remember the night she sat up late
while he was battling the pneumonia, writing
his obituary: *John was a man of simple pleasures*
detailing all she knew needed to be said.
He loved his family, his home, his garden . . .

Always, it was her voice luring me toward song,
reciting poems to me—no doubt in the womb.
That morning just before he died, I woke
to her weeping beside me, asked what
she was feeling. She chanted her reply:

The time has come to say goodbye
I cannot speak, I cannot cry . . .

Time creeps too fast to go . . .
Soul is where—I want to know

Is he there, does he hear?
Does he know what I fear?

Is it only despair—
to wonder what is there?

So today I link the golden eagles' wind literacy
to the notebooks we found preparing his sickroom:
pages of rhymed verse—hers, from high school.
She has not written a poem since I was born.
Perhaps she's finally remembered the currents.
That morning in bed I heard her cry:

I have so much to live, so much to say.

Their Voices

The heat—the close of another August day.
I rummage drawers of half-sleep for the voices
of my three aunts, lest time erase
the special timbre of their speech: the way

Ann's laughter endures, despite the din
of a decade's chatter, erupts in raspy
bursts—gin fizz from a barkeep's
wand. Her Lucky Strike aloft. Then

Flo died. Yet I still hear that twang
in her vowels, the wah-wah of a trumpet
solo at the Sons of Italy dance. Last, let
Ginny's cigarillo tones request a tango.

My memory's the vessel—an old jar, lid
punched with holes, to let the fireflies live.

Teresa, Crossing Over

Our last visit: her space shrunk to one room on the dementia hall,
      behind a locked door. A few family photos on the dresser,
a smiling Pope Francis on the wall.
                          I see thoroughbreds galloping in a field
behind a split rail fence, chestnut and bay flanks glistening in the August sun.

Her eyes stare straight ahead, as if she could see into the next room—
      cloud light, and familiar faces around a table, calling her in . . .

I picture a great blue heron on a rock beside a stream,
      spreading its full wingspan as if it would lift off,
as if it were opening its being to the sun's light.

Her lips are parched; I offer only cracked ice. She asks me: *Are we going yet?*
      Then answers: *soon now,* as if I am no longer there.

Outside the window, the sudden ascent of a tiger swallowtail
      from the coneflowers, aroma of nectar in its feet.

Sustenance

Which of you, if your child asked for bread,
would give him a stone?
—Matthew 7:9

I.

That first weekend in Intensive Care,
among the horror-movie particulars:
the ventilator hose lifts, like an alien's tentacle,
forcing breath through airways
choked with pneumonia.

Then beneath his elevated chin,
my father's southpaw script on the clipboard:
    I love you.
When do I get off this thing?
        Sports page . . .

———————

Quickly the doctors dictate
our choices: as soon as he's off,
he needs to know the risks of eating.

My sister riffs
on Durkheim's Law: all the new "choices"—
driftwood in technology's wake.

———————

Meanwhile, we learn about the bacteria
of pneumonia, like the varieties of crabgrass:
this aspiration kind knows no weed killer;
anaerobic bacteria have yet to meet
their match in the antibiotic realm.

And so he re-enters the world
breathing but not eating. Fed, yes—
first with IV fluids, and then via
tube and pump: the nutrient-rich brew
that would extend his life.

II.

Observe the lilies of the field—
the red geranium in the pot,
the swamp maple in the backyard—
they do not toil or reap,
yet they draw sustenance . . .

> Had anyone told me that this man,
> devotee of ice cream and meatloaf,
> black & white milkshakes, bacon & eggs
> over easy, would survive this loss—

Think of it: he is up,
able to walk and visit, pet
the cat and watch baseball.
But no hotdogs and beer, no
TastyKakes—no Holy Communion.

———

> So tiny gestures become sacraments:
> swabbing his dry mouth, applying cream
> to lips thinned from weeks without food
> or drink, delicate as when he and I nursed
> a downed nestling in a shoebox.

Dew on a blade of grass, a few
creamy blossoms on the gardenia,
    the rusty flash of a robin's wing
at the window—can the other
    senses ever offset this loss?

III.

Nearly a year for him to weigh
this new existence. Against his wishes
we deny ourselves, try to relish with him:

    sweet scent
    from *that scraggly bush*—
    white roses

                    ship's clock chimes
                    sparrow chatter in the fig tree
                        last fruit

    October sun
    breeze shifting
    the maple's shade

                    dipping the swab
                    in Communion wine—
                    for New Year's, ginger ale

Through it all, how he urges us: savor
all that sustains you, partake for me—
the flesh of new tomatoes, yeasty first bites
of cinnamon buns fresh from the oven,
hot coffee on the palate.

His Thanksgiving grace: *bless us*
O Lord, for these Thy gifts, that THEY
are about to receive . . .

IV.

Impossible in the end
for us to deny all that bound us to him
      around a common table,
for him to accept the separation
      (only a drop of wine, never the host)
despite the blessing of time—

    Do you know, he asked,
    after the speech therapist
    allowed him a spoonful
    of tapioca as a trial, *what it's like*
    to taste after ten months?

My brother still swears
    that on Ash Wednesday
Dad tilted the cup in the hands
    of the Eucharistic minister
and took a full gulp—*only say the Word*
    and my soul shall be healed.

---

    at the funeral home
    his First Communion photograph
    votive-lit

Pruning the Rhododendron

Dead branches waiting for the axe
since winter's weight of snow. Mother
sighs: *your father gave up, he'd rather
cut it down.* I contemplate the facts:

planted to christen their new home
fifty years ago, it nearly surmounts
the roof. Since his first pneumonia bout,
new fists of purple have begun to bloom—

starbursts on withering limbs. Weigh
this: one should wait until the blossoms die.
Still I grab the lopper, channel all my
intention, releasing each dry bough

onto a growing pile. *For your penance
a decade. . . . Thy will*—endurance.

Conversation, Interrupted

> *"In one of the stars, I shall be living,*
> *in one of them I shall be laughing. . . ."*
> —Antoine de Saint-Exupéry

I.

A scene, painted on the wall of a Brussels inn—
invitation to re-enter the world of *Le Petit Prince*:
I am twelve   twenty-one   loving the fox, the rose
       the lamplighter.
I am fifty-nine, wishing I *were* the rose, on my planet—
able to hear my father's laughter, his one-register
too-loud baritone   in the chapel   on the street
       among the stars.

Once I wrote a poem about my father's intolerance
of silence, his stage-bred need to provide
color commentary for any mundane errand in the car.
Then, I'd have paid a hefty sum to silence him. Today,
I'd rob a bank to hear him call me in from play.

II.

In the emergency room, he was bored
               and without glasses. So I read to him—
the sports page: *Phillies manager's contract extended,*
             and carefully skimmed "the bad news" he'd rue daily.
His habitual quip: *The world's a mess.*
The last night I heard that voice, hoarse from the oxygen,
and suctioning, he sang to mother one more refrain:
Have I told you lately that I love you?
Then: *I'm dying . . .* looking her in the eye.
We're all dying, her reply.

Later while she slept, he told me in a whisper
to take care of her, to look out for my brother.
Then for three days, silence—a beatific smile
          when we sang familiar hymns,
and for his favorite showtunes, a raised eyebrow.
Toward the end, only breath—

The Work

—your words, reverent, and wide enough to include
neighborhood gang leaders and priests who
minister at altar and pub, the doorstep conversations
to build a case for change and the rowdy negotiations—
these church folks tuning spirituals and labor anthems
up for the Cintas Corp suits today. A feisty nun's
making a case for the locked-out workers
as I recall *your* actions louder than words.

Still at it during lucid spells in the Little Sisters of Mercy
hospice, you were cooking up one more campaign, thirsty
to call the health care machine to account for holding
you with vulnerable millions in its maw. You, molding
strategies as if the tumors in your brain were fed
by the persistent spark—that imagination cultivated
at beat-up tables in storefront offices, and till all hours
in whosever pad you were crashing. The powers

too well organized for us to rest from pressing slumlords
into compliance, so tenants used to rats would learn to forge
their own power and challenge aldermen, zoning boards,
and bankers whose fiat could wave jobs or neighborhoods
away quicker than a magician's sleight of hand. If not
for the breed of organizer you pulled from your hat,
and prodded into a thousand acts of resistance. *Action,*
you taught, *the lifeblood of a peoples' organization.*

Again, I hear your voice in the voice of Vern Sloan, fourth
generation farmer in Stryker, Ohio, wondering if it's worth
the fight, whether at eighty-two he should call out the Justice
boys on Archer Daniels Midland for locking up the price
of corn which might force his livestock farmer son to sell
a farm that's been in the family since 1835. Well . . .

he wants to know from me, should he raise a ruckus,
just so his grandson learns how the world works.

In memoriam, Tom Gaudette,
Community Organizer and teacher (1924–1999)

Requiem at Compline

—for K.S. (1952–2000)

When I heard that you had died, I found
a deserted beach to make my peace with you.
We skirted sandpiper tracks, full moon
illuminating the tidepools around
our long running tango. The wash of waves
dissolved the last echoes of your confession,
cleared the musty relics of each transgression
I harbored, softened the hair shirt you wove
of small kindnesses over the years. Now
I imagine you above our bickering
voices, redeemed at last from doctors
and dialysis, free to ramble, to dowse
in a philosopher's realm, spirits flickering
in amity, without this need for words.

Waking Heaney in Edgartown, Massachusetts

I.

Joe Creedon says he learned of Heaney's death
from the bread man. First off, where but
rural Ireland do they still have bread
men? And second, as Joe Creedon puts
it, "how fitting" that the bread man
would be mourning Seamus, too. I'm half
a world away, yet I hear them keen
in the bog: black sheep heads lift;
a harrowing wind stirs the bracken;
bog lakes dishevel with cloud scuttle.
I first glean from my own husband
the poet's last words, left in Latin.
Here, Heaney's vowels bid me: *head up*
into the dock fog. Oracle, ploughman.

II.

So Seamus, I tramp Edgartown, your book
in my bag, your verses thick in mind
on the day of your home-going. I pluck
names, hear *you* intone: *Nora's Lane,*
Bittersweet Farm, Summer Road,
salute a stone wall or two beneath
some ferns. It's September now,
less light, more likely this scenery
would yield up ghosts. But where?
A ragweed field—fluff. No *squelch*
and slap of soggy peat, heather and hay
scented. Your revenant would require
a brume, *banked cloud.* You said yourself:
a man—truly wise . . . knows his dark places.

III.

Here among the four trunks of the zelkova
the laureate appears—vigorous, nested
as in the oak of the old photo. Sure, his ghost
frequents graveyards, like the one sign-posted
on Beara, Cork: "Grave digging is dangerous . . .
and should not be undertaken by unapproved
persons." So the locals mourn the lost rasp
of shovel and trowel angled into the clotted
earth. Such offices bless the ground. My own
father wanted to be laid into the sod,
not entombed in casket and stone. He'd not
get that wish. Where Heaney lies, at home,
the graves bloom: fuchsia, pennywort, gorse—
hand planted in devotion, resistance.

II
Lumen de Lumine

Twilight, Ardgroom

Bumping along in the backseat of a van,
we pilgrims watch nubs of granite
strewn across Beara hillsides, see waves
crash over skelligs and stone beaches.
Scrubby tufts of grasses, a knobby yew
or two and palm fronds rustle as we pass.

At Ardgroom, the bog-soggy climb
across fields and over laddered fences
ascending to the ancient circle of stones.
Angelus hour. The rays transform
us into seven new strokes of shadow
moving among tines cast already
for three thousand years of days. Heedless
of us, a larger circle of ewes and lambs
bray their offering out. Incense altar,
smoke and scent rising from this odd
patch: pilgrims, stones, grasses, mud—
all earth. I finger the water-worn,
lichened stones one by one, lay
hands on the warmth of all nine
left standing.
             Now mind the spirit
of whosoever hands erected this:
kil, cashel, timepiece, sacred space.
Here our elements strike ancestral flint.
Moon and star shine, bonfires, all
have lit this height, stirred air
that sanctifies wells, cairns,
Kenmare waters, ourselves—
touched, tethered, aglow.

This Far

*having come this far
alive at fifty-five:
the morning star*
　　　　　—Nick Virgilio

I.

sometimes a journey begins

this way

paddling into lilies

into clouds

you survive

a fear that pounds

like your footsteps

on the forest floor

the first maples

turning red—

intimations of autumn

you always knew

you would round this bend

a patch of river grass

impedes your stroke,

glistening, it rustles

within your reflection

rippling clouds

breathing in, you observe

the impermanence of

all dharmas

morning sunlight

a loon on the lake

in the shallows

bleached to bone

a downed pine

wind-sculpted

Adirondack pines

at the ridge top

water lily pad

red against yellow—

the lotus' center

gnarled tree shanks

mark the channel into

a beaver's lodge

beside the lotus

sun spot, tree shadow

among choke weed

a great blue heron turns

white cloud

climbing

blue mountain

II.

alive yes, and grateful
to be surfacing on a woodland
footbridge, logs placed across
the muddy parts, dappled sunlight
on the ferns, my footsteps setting off
an ignition of wings, before I sense
a presence close enough to feel its breath—
the wary gaze of a doe at eye level
measuring my step
                              ill-advised,
surely not altogether safe, this sunset
hike, but something compelled me
to bait the trap, and walk into
the realm of my own nightmare:
tangled roots, fatigue and no one
within earshot
                         for no good reason
except to prove I will not live into
a life forecast by some genetic throw
of the dice, each day a new foreboding,
instead seek my own reckoning
in the scent of early autumn
sun inciting pine needles
to bear each footfall, sweeter
still in their state of decay

III.

Talk of comet dust, naming
          constellations, echoes out
over the August-chilled lake

this shower of pebble-sized debris
          our planet's been traversing
for centuries, and we're still fifteen million

miles off, cycling back into the tail.
          So here we are spinning
through the brilliant litter, waiting

for a spark, aching to levitate on one
          dancing filament, to break free
of crickets, this great camp, the thin

incense of words, into the meteors' arc
          of praise, dust too, and shining.

Lumen de Lumine

I.

February, and I'm in flight from the frigid streets
        of Paris in search of illumination,

enter tiny Sainte Chapelle, its fifteen arched verrières
      two rosettes
                 such artistry—turning Gothic stone
into lanterns of light.

Eleven hundred thirteen illustrated scenes,
      individual vitrines, crafted to instruct the faithful.

What of the anonymous creators, through whose hands
      —sand and wood ash, blown & molten glass—
          light   is transformed?

II.

Monet created his gardens first, called them a lyric poem
      with water and willows   —   the first nymphéas.
He watched boundaries blur between   sky   earth   water
      dapples of blossom   spreading green   lotus
      exploding   sun stroke
annulling shore   horizon   conjuring his own palette
      as the elements interpenetrated—
                molecules   in space   miraculous
inversion:
        Le ciel à mes pieds!   *Les saules flottants!*

III.

In two tennis court-sized rooms, built to house eight *Nymphéas*,
L'Orangerie assembled Monet's "rêverie flottante,"
just months after his death at eighty-six.

Twenty years from first brush to finished canvasses,
　　　his obsession survived the loss of wife and son,
The Great War—the energy of his moving arm
　　　became his feverish, mute rebuke.

　　　　　　　Then the cataracts, and his urgency
to liberate light　　　　　—　　　　and hold it, for eight more years.

IV.

Imagine gathering thousands of stained-glass artisans
　　　in such a space　　　　　　to capture their collective
reflection　　　like the multiplication of *Nymphéas*,
　　　or like quaking aspen—hundreds of acres, one shimmering.

Have Monet interrogate them, each with a tiny episode
　　　to render:　　　　　Eve in the garden,
　　　　　　Moses at the Red Sea,
　　　Elijah in the Valley of Dry Bones,
　　　　　　Jesus in the Garden,
　　　Thomas putting his hand in Jesus' side,
　　　　　　St. Helena discovering the Cross,
　　　St. Louis receiving the Crown of Thorns
　　　　　　from returning Crusaders.

We can barely see the thousands of carefully wrought lessons
　　　their handiwork　　where it looms in Gothic arches.

They added ash and oxides to globs of molten glass,
       blew a bubble into a gather of it,
      spun out cobalt, green, or orange panes
         in cylinders of wood
      then heat   cold   until they sculpted
        lumens   into eternities of lead.

The Gleaners

Their uplifted faces, rapt before Millet's masterpiece, as their docent explains the economics behind the scene—how thoroughly the tiny men in the background would have harvested the piles of tares at the women's feet, how they would have bundled their gleanings. The little ones offer their teacher eager answers about what one does with *blé,* volunteering *gâteaux* before *pain quotidien.* Yet this is Paris 2011—enough immigrant faces among them to know something about hunger, and gathering all that's left after even meager harvests . . .

> February rain
> beneath the rose window
> votives flicker

At the Mariner's Chapel, Auvillar

St. Catherine carved in white marble, vigils
over the remains of a church once filled
with grateful gifts from sailors who thanked her
for their safe return. Today between a timbered ceiling
and the cool embrace of undecorated granite
mysterious landscape paintings grace the walls.
Scenes of fog, with dark hints of mast or bow,
yellow orbs that suggest sun, brown brush strokes
of bird feather, impressions of distorted angel wings.
The artist is reading a book. I approach to ask him,
myself perhaps too, how much of what has emerged
to shimmer indistinct on these canvases, was born
of clear intent, how much the random encounter
of paint and canvas—an emergence, absent
the strong arm of will. Where, I wonder, has the ego
yielded lines to shadowing, a palette of sun
and gathering clouds into feathering, flight. His reply,
tossed like a pebble echoes: *does it not all come
from the void?* Myself, at the well's rim, listening.

Illumination

*The continuous process of remaining open and accepting of what may
reveal itself through hand and heart on a crafted page is the closest
I have ever come to God.*
                    —Donald Jackson, calligrapher, *St John's Bible*

I.

The Raven is the Messenger

A life's work: blending chroma from Minnesota bog lichen and gorse hues
            of his native heath—
Gestation in ribbons of chaos, spirit flowering into moons and turquoise sea.
            Shards of the godhead hovering over it all.

How does one give oneself, not to the years mastering the stroke
            and the scriptorium's offices,
but to contemplation   listening for the voice in Lectio that calls
            for *this* wildflower pigment, *that* sheen of a crow's feather,
the distinct shape of a butterfly or bee
            in the margin   to break open some long obscure versicle?
*Did they suppose that either fire or wind, or swiftness or the circle of stars
            or the turbulent air . . .*
would shine forth   illuminated?

II.

The Scribe's Art

First task: to create an alphabet of ink—lampblack
            dissolved in honey and water, or black walnut oil and an egg

40

yolk pierced with a pen knife. The duck or goose feathers,
    first stripped and boiled, need to be hand cut
to perfect the shape and angle of each nib, so the ink will flow
    into letters. Then the scribe's art: invent the exact script,
shapes meant not for royal proclamation, but
    to carry The Word into a world grown resistant.
This maestro knows monastic foundations gone to ruin
    on islands, riverbanks and hills of Europe, where monks
with cramped hands crafted annals to mesmerize the faithful. This
    commission is meant to crack the Word open, invite
        new eyes in.

III.

Valley of Dry Bones
    And you O mortal, take a brick and set it before you. On it portray a city. . . .
        —Ezekiel 4:1

And so, on the brink of a new century, the queen's calligrapher
    devotes a decade and more to this, sets out
with an archeologist's eye to unearth artifacts, resurrect
    the prophet's ire: *mortal, can these bones live*—
        in the Rwandan machetes' aftermath
beside the rotting corpses of men and boys in the shallow graves
    of Srebrenica   within the craters of "Daisy Cutters"
in the Afghan mountains.

Your sharpened quill must have hesitated among the heaped skulls
    in the Valley of Dry Bones.
In what mad state did you dare to fling shards of gold leaf
    so that we the witnesses glimpse our own spark   of divinity there?

We who did not stay the hand of the murderers
    or lay our own bodies before the tanks
        bought and paid for   with Caesar's gold.
Your search, born of egg yolk and blood root   sets vellum afire.

IV.

As Abraham's Oblation

Only vellum, created the old way—
    skin of a stillborn goat prized for smoothness
soaked in lime, scraped clean with a curved knife,
    stretched and sanded, buffed—would receive
the ink, careful strokes of each calligrapher.
        Then a few charged with illuminating: apply burnished gold leaf,
plummet with gesso, honey and glue. Grind malachite,
    lapis and verdigris with calcinated chicken bone.
Extract powder with lye and resins to make the bright-hued paint
    that will explode into panels for the seven days of Creation.
Cornflowers, poppy and iris, violets and bilberry bound to powder
        from crushed seashells, will release the inner light
from David's harp and slingshot, the Ark, Rachel weeping
    for her children, the Baptist's desert proclamation.
In ink and pigment, these hands unleash, in Father Hopkins' words:
    the dearest freshness deep down, onto the goatskin page.

V.

The End is the Beginning

Rounding the last bend
       the theologians are debating Revelation—how it will be cast.
The master illuminator   seems stumped,
       suspended on the plains of Armageddon. Too much
          Weaponry that defies depiction   Chaos   that might annihilate All:
              Holy Books   the landscape's palette
           what pulse remains   of the Divine   in the rubble,
               in the albumen of a hen's egg.

In the Benedictine priory's womb
two carved Tablets of Welsh Oak   await

          ∞

        breath
   lettering   the last
     brushstrokes.

Museum of Divine Statues

The make-up artist with a Celtic tattoo
has a soft spot for orphaned statues.
It started with a damaged St. Clare of Assisi
in an antique store. He took her home.
So when the tidal wave of church closings
rolled through Cleveland, Ohio, he started
adopting: Our Lady of Grace, St. Therese
the Little Flower from the shuttered St. Hyacinth
parish, St. Francis of Assisi from Lorain,
St. Stephen from Margaret of Hungary
in Chagrin Falls. Chagrin indeed.

Now the ladies of a certain age line up
to visit the *Museum of Divine Statues*
in the old St. Hedwig's complex—a steal
for $200K—rectory and school thrown in.
Think of all the prayers whispered
in many languages over the years,
muses the curator-restorer. It's become
a family affair, though his sainted father
confides that some of the glassy-eyed saints
freak him out. Imagine this sanctuary
after closing time: St. Jude enumerating
his lost causes all night in the basement,
Our Lady of Mount Carmel lamenting
St. Patrick's dislodged miter and chipping
snakes, a wingless angel searching in vain
for what has been lost.

Roots, Exposed

I.

Towpath, Washington, DC

Above a narrow berth on the far bank
of Rock Creek, winters' bouts of storm
have unsheathed a maple's spindly roots.
Stripped of earth, bleached of hue
and mossy cover, it angles out
over an unstable jut of what was once
its ground and sustenance. Gone the web—
cellulose and lignin, sap and circulation
that breathed: *tree, truth, truce.*

II.

Sierra, near Truckee, CA

Angr, from the Norse—grief, loss. A slow
erosion, like the raging creek, rerouted
by earthmovers and fill, condominiums
and the scream of macadam, where once
Washoe women gathered bulbs, their infants
resting on manzanita shrub. Water slicing through
granite, granular—canyon.

III.

Observe the slow burn: a prone
Virginia pine decomposes for all to see.
A beetle army has ravaged here. Hieroglyphic
trace of their tunneling, grievous fungal trail.

White fir saplings hug old-growth pine—
implicit intimacy—again and again
this message: *What's next?* (his last words) . . .
                    a different forest.

Fault Lines

I.

Three moonless nights
      since a full moon and the Southern Cross
illuminated our two figures descending narrow trails of schist
          from Rangitoto's now-forested crater.

Fifty extinct volcanos in Hauraki Gulf alone.
      Undersea plates still collide over fault lines
where mountain ranges emerged
      as if carved by adze-wielding warriors.

We're fingering New Zealand's topography
      in Maori artifacts   and stone encampments
the raised letters of whalebone.

II.

Only two bat genii and ancient tree ferns
      rode the breakaway ridge   an iceberg-sized castaway
      from the great Southern land mass Gondwana.
Rats and dogs first arrived on Polynesian canoes.
      In less than three hundred years.
the Maori hunted the moa to extinction.   Only three decades
      for the Maori to succumb to European diseases.

III.

Beneath the inverted sword of Orion in Otaga:
       relics of Irish penal colony escapees,
the first to intermarry and learn these seas.
       Fur seals and sperm whale would pay the price.

Water chemically alters the face of limestone over centuries.
       Pakeha took even less time to leave our mark.

            Nine horsemen ford the stream at Arrowtown.
               Lamb tails are ringed; it's spring in Glenorchy.

It may only take a tremor   or an ice melt
       to provoke the next cataclysm.

Irruption

Though accurate, the clinical word
does no justice to the debut of a bird
that before I'd only known from poets
invoking white wings over winter fields,
the quick menacing dagger of shadow
overtaking a mouse or rabbit
that never had a chance.
                                    This winter,
I'm hunting for a glimpse of the majestic
white bird perched on a hotel entrance
awning or drugstore marquis, as thousands
of snowy owls irrupt southward
from the lemming-rich Arctic to alight
on Delmarva wetlands, the Chesapeake Bay
Bridge, New Jersey's Famous Steel Pier—
wherever a frozen expanse of water,
grass or asphalt telegraphs: *tundra.*

A now-famous female snowy owl
rescued from downtown traffic
is wintering over at an undisclosed location.
That bird grew agitated in captivity,
her handlers rejoicing at the slightest sign
of recovery from the stupor of poison-laced
rodents she'd fed on, a diet that landed her
in the path of a city bus and an SUV.
She'll soon be released into the wild
like the bird in the *Times* photo—
wings extended into a V at the end
of a ranger's arm—eyes glinting
like coals, like Hamlet's father's ghost.

That owl rocketed off into a whirling
pas-de-deux with another Arctic voyager,
before vanishing as if to rejoin
some mythic journey. What insight
shall we glean from these visitations?
Threat or warning, a chance
to glimpse the invincible
so fragile among us.

Heist

Mt. St. Angelo, VA

I.

The bay horse trots into a universe of birds—

> *auto exhaust, train whistle and thrust; into a realm*
>> *where chicken wire ignites with lasers, cricket chant.*

A high-spirited chestnut snorts, annoyed by this intrusion, insistent flies—
tail slap, whinny . . . then the two head off into the meadow

> *October sun glints on haunches, horsetails*
>> *flicking out into traffic hum over the ridge top.*

II.

If *hope is the thing with feathers*, Emily, in what language does it speak?

Deception colonizes this hilltop.
Impossible to discern the original *tu-ee, tu-ee* of the rufous-sided towhee,
Northern cardinal *chee, chee,* or sparrow arpeggio
in its original key, when a flock
of mockingbirds transpose it all into their high decibel diatribe,
flashy imitation of avian sonata.

Still eavesdropping's ubiquitous here:
poets, composers, hungry for sound bits, abound . . .
better them than national intelligence omnivores.

III.

Try as they might, two inspired sound sculptors
have so far failed to incite a trans-species duet;
no efficient means to seduce the melody of September
crickets. Strands of human hair flailing catgut
of banjo—even flute as snake conjurer, keyboard
or ukulele notes can only mimic, not entice . . .
Yet, after dark, the crickets' mezzo solo surrounds
the illuminated sphere—scree, star shower.

IV.

You have to get in close here,
for the sound of cows munching
tough meadow grass to be audible.
I'm trying to re-create the granite silence
of a Beara boreen where, despite the baffle
of fuchsia hedge, blackberry briar, that
rhythmic bass line—a herd of dairy cows
chewing their cud—would accompany
the crunch of gravel, hidden stream music
underlining the native stillness.

V.

The first real dose of quiet in these
Blue Ridge foothills, where traffic and talk
can drown out history: plantation remnants
out over the dammed lake. Here,
a dying ash tree's the omphalos, hiving
flies to a slave graveyard. The new plaque
calls them "founders," to what is now a pricey
private college. Indeed, their sweat
laid stones, planted corn and tobacco,
ground flour, tended cows and mowed
the meadows to feed livestock. And the cost—

I kick aside the first piles of autumn
leaves to uncover the granite stubs of old
grave markers, huddled as if against rain,
remembrance. What names shall we give
them, what incense burn in honor, expiation?
I join the remnant congregation: tiger
swallowtail, catbird, foraging squirrel,
and whisper a belated Kaddish. I pour
a few drops of water, watch libation
glisten on this insufficient memorial.

Christ Crucified at Our Savior Church in LA

He is muscular, this Jesus
on the chapel cross—sinews and
biceps pulsing with the energy
of a Michelangelo Adonis.
The massive crucifix must weigh
three tons. It shouts to be seen,
suspended over the altar, under
the great dome—echo of an era
more triumphant. My eyes drift up
from the consecration to his agony.
He's not quite resisting, but the body
and its nimble shadows, cast like
the two thieves, one to each side, press
away from the wood, as if this Jesus
might just leap off into the crowd.

A laborer, perhaps of Mexican descent
must have modeled for this Christ,
no lean, patrician savior. He reminds me
of my friend George, son of a Greek
immigrant who ran a New Jersey diner,
and who never stops lifting, laughing—energy
moving through space. The last I saw him
we were boxing up the house of a friend
for his move to a nursing home. George stops
to load up and heave bags of fresh fruit and
vegetables, so that Tony will eat well.
That same physical strength exudes
from this Christ. He's no compliant,
passive sufferer, but embodied, so
we *feel* his humanity giving out.
I believe today he'd be with George

at the nursing home, double ordering
chocolate ice cream for Tony, cajoling
the nurses. Christ bounding into the fray.

Riff: *what it takes*

It takes a lot of energy to digest dead things.
Mushrooms are better at it than humans
although we do our share of creating carrion.
Funky fungi set up shop on a downed redwood
or juniper and pretty soon these champignons
balloon into a full jazz orchestra—fleshy moons,
a whole solar system of spores, transposing wood
into an all-you-can-eat insect pantry buffet.
Honey bees have it down when it comes
to thermal bliss. These tropical transplants
haul pollen protein home to feed their larvae.
Once the hive is *bummin'*, the queen and her drones
start to shiver (*all together now*), and that cosmic
vibration lasts all winter, gyrating just enough
heat to warm all the pupae, and generate
the sweet by-product—*mmm honey!*

> aspen flashing
> the afternoon sun

Hummingbirds are downright calculating.
Can't waste energy when those wings beat
eighty times a second, hovering over the scarlet
gilea. With only one sip at the bottom
of each blossom, *hummingbird's gotta run*
complex equations to syncopate her visit
to each bed of impatiens, each cluster
of red-yellow columbine on the forest floor,
all the while reserving the best serving
at the center of that territory she hoards
with all her might.

at the podium
sunset—in a vase
of wildflowers

Summer is siesta time for conifers. Just watch
those Jeffreys shed branches for efficiency, note
the angle of the lodgepoles waiting to catch
the metric slant of the winter sun's rays.
Just now, they're all juicin' on the *e*
they've trapped and gotten down
to mushroom cilia who feed the mycorrhiza
that let the tree conduct H_2O from its roots
ensemble to harmonize thousands of needles.

Now tell me again Shakespeare:
what a piece of work—?

dawn light
pulsing, a tiger butterfly
smells a leaf

Walking the Elements, Beara Peninsula

I have walked the body transparent.
—Nan Shepherd

I.

Moss, sod, earth underfoot,
descending into the hazel wood,
I caress each tree's bark, birch
smooth as leather and lichened fir,
detect a common pulse beneath
my palm and underfoot that leads
me deeper. The muddy crust thins
as I acknowledge all that's within
me, tangled as the tendrils of hazel
meandering toward the water table.
Siphon in and up this breath,
drawn from below: sister earth's
green-brown tingling. No threat
in this descent. An invitation to rest.

II.

This, the breath I was born for:
streams of mist condense into
a waterfall of ch'i, like an Irish air
passing over the lips' ledge, and out
to join the ubiquitous Beara duet—
rushing streams and cascades' crescendo.
Here, feel the *will* of water, having at
rock from every angle. Caught
in the drift, one hazel leaf, unharried,
until a swift current sends it rolling
off, over the low rocks and down.

I'm with O'Donohue, wanting to *become*
water—this stream, *carried*
by the surprise of its own unfolding.

III.

On a day with little sun, hazy
cloud and mist descending over
Miskish, I'm left to *conjure* fire.
Glimpses of montbretia, blazing
orange stars along the lanes, mix
with dandelion in flower, purple phlox
and hydrangea—brilliant even in rain.
Along the lanes, heads of hay wave
subtly in the Coulagh breeze. Still
time to stir the embers, ash to flame
in me. Like a low peat fire,
sods reddening but not yet ablaze.
Only breath, held at the heart center
may kindle inspiration, will.

IV.

[JOT 1928–2011]

Since you left us, I've relived
your last breath, over and over—
the sight of your head drooped,
inanimate. Here on Beara, my own
breath brought back the moment,
an intimate connection to the air,
and to your spirit that still surrounds
us. Each day your breath, your
atoms reform in our lungs, on our

lips, in our blood. Your song
still wants to be heard, if only
I can listen, and hold the notes
you leave me, make of that
melody my own refrain.

III
What Kind of Silence

At the First Canonical Hour

A single Jeffrey Pine rises out of the darkness, as if lifting an oblation of stars,
trunk studded like a gemmed chalice.

In the midnight silence: flutter of a moth's wing, the earth's exhalation of
        cedar,
heated pine sap and sagebrush—a psalm lingering on the mountain.

The marbled sky, delicate as the inside of an eggshell, dark tips of lodgepole pines
casting their shadows up as a circle of unlit candles.

Only the flickering of airplane lights—distant fireflies, Morse code strokes—
hints at our presence in this sanctuary.

What acknowledgment shall we make on entering?

What mantra or penance for the blood beneath our fingernails, before we pray:

     for the blessing of sleep

                          now I lay me

     for the earth's bounty, we've kept

                          down to sleep

     from the children [Haiti, Congo] who'll

                          die before I wake

     grieve in stillness

                          soul to keep

     resolve: honor

                          soul to take

     this offering.

On the Feast of St. Francis, Transitus

A canvas of dawn sky, a stand of yew
and ash, soundtrack of mixed birdsong,
October crickets. First up: a pair of high fliers
crossing north, stray geese perhaps—indistinct
from this distance. Then a brilliance erupts
in a brief contrail of southbound jet—
luminous snail, cloud hyphen.
From the valley, the clatter of freight on rails
bisects the scene, for a moment, drowning out
the crickets. Strips of lavender mist appear,
and seem to separate sound from light
until the sun crests the far ridge to reveal
two horses in the field, backlit, tails like torches.
What souls this morning will exit this world
of such particular pleasures?

Parable

His name is John, dapper in denim jacket
and shades, standing with his white cane
at the entrance to the Union Station Metro,
where he greets streams of commuters
he can only hear passing by: *Good morning!*
Good morning! Feeling their busy breeze.
For once today, I have time, take time
to stop, to talk to John, find out who he is
and ask what brings him to the station.
Life's been hard . . . but I'm not bitter, he offers.
Turns out he came up north from Carolina
decades ago. In ninety-eight, he was working
on his car, when the battery exploded,
blinding him in both eyes. Now I notice
the scars. He wants to know my name.
Though he's not holding out a cup, or asking
for spare change, I press a few bills into his palm:
for coffee. He insists on giving me a hug
with thanks for stopping, though I don't know
why I did, on this particular day.
I've always loved the parable of Jesus
and Bartimaeus, how in Mark's account
the blind beggar calls out, makes a ruckus
so Jesus and the disciples could not miss
seeing him. Jesus assumes nothing,
instead takes the time to ask the man:
What do you want me to do for you?
Bartimaeus' reply: *Teacher, I want*
to see. So, in the end, Jesus credits
the blind man with the miracle.

Bop: The Truth and Nothing But—

This morning it was buried beneath the fold,
page three, in a story about some declassified
documents. It turns out, the FBI had questioned
the deposed dictator just before he was hanged.
It turns out he had destroyed those weapons
after the last war. His take on Al Qaeda—*fanatics.*

What kind of voice is breaking silence, what kind
of silence is being broken?

The landscape painter traveled to ten states,
North and South, his brush conjuring the spirits
in trees. On his canvas, disturbing trees: centennial
oak, large-limbed in shade, twisted remains
of an old cypress at the crossroads, a gnarled
ash by the whitewashed courthouse—all hint
at their history with disfigurement, haunting
as if the mangled weight still hangs there.

What kind of voice is breaking silence, what kind
of silence. . .

Among morning commuters on the Metro, the rant
of a homeless vet, one minute recalling carpet bombs
in 'Nam, the next pivoting to defend: *They can't take us!*
America. In his voice the fervor of a street corner
preacher calling down eternal fire for our sins, so easy
to dismiss as one more lunatic, but for what we know . . .

What kind of voice is breaking . . . what kind of silence?

Halim, Waiting

He arrived first as a student of geology
        in the bicentennial year.
                            He witnessed
the fireworks, read the Declaration and believed it.

One by one, he brought his family—Fahima, Anas,
        Nassir. Today they are all citizens. He alone waits.

He built houses, a business, this dream. Eighteen years
        of waiting to savor the meat he first smelled roasting

on Manhattan streets. His father's home in Baghdad
        is in ruins. The cousins in Najaf are dead, conscripted—

His youngest son has brought the daughter of a family friend
        to Virginia to marry. Even she will be a citizen before him.

Each time he travels home, one more letter in his file
        for helping the war effort.

                        Still at each airport, the pat-downs,
pull asides, manhandling—the eyes.

                        At the immigration office
they say: one more name check. One more set of fingerprints.

His wife says: *Now they will not give this. They need to keep him*
        on this leash.

Lauds, Aberdeen Creek

First hints of sunrise
appear in cloud script
on Aberdeen inlet, scattered
with the shrill of osprey
fledglings awaiting the hunter's
return. A few boats at anchor
yet no one's stirring. This
is the grateful hour.

The ripple of a fish
beneath the matte green
waters attracts the osprey
parent, its high-pitched squawk
a twirling lasso until
it scissors down
into one angled and accurate
splash. Somewhere,

in a monastery, they
are chanting Lauds.
Somewhere up the creek
a waterman's skiff purrs
its wake above the bottom
crawlers, arranging its trail
of bait, waiting. I'll wait

for the great blue
heron to drift down,
wings arced toward the east,
as if to honor the light.
No one of us owns
this dawn, pink and unbidden
but each, in its own tongue
can articulate
praise.

Starlings

The children swarm outside
the supermarket, arms flailing,
their high-pitched exclamations
surround me, my own arms laden
with groceries. My mind suddenly shifts
to tally one week's arithmetic of grief:
eighty children among the hundreds killed
in a fine-tuned cone of shrapnel,
three siblings on a Gaza rooftop
before the missile landed, and four
cousins on a beach incinerated
in the time it takes me to close the car door.
Tonight, the trees are full of starlings.
Their racket rising into a delicate
tremolo, like in that Bernstein *Sonata*
for Violin that stretches the strings
almost to breaking.

Witness

Willie Reed (1937–2013)

In this year of Civil Rights retrospection,
a name: Willie Reed, unknown to me until
his death, the haunting details of his story
appear on the front page. At eighteen,
Willie dared to testify, dared to tell
an all-white jury what he saw and heard
that night in Money, Mississippi.

That August night, exactly eight years
before Dr. King's dream would echo out
from Lincoln's columns over the thousands
who marched, Willie happened to be walking
to the store when he saw the pick-up truck,
just happened to see the same truck parked
by Milam's cousin's barn, just happened
to hear young Emmet Till . . . *hollering . . .*
and some licks . . . a whole lot of them . . .
like somebody was whipping somebody.

Till's cousin remembers: *for him to testify*
against those men, that was instant death . . .
Pure terror. You had to live those times to even know.
The prosecutor recalls Reed's barely audible
voice in court: *Took more nerve than I have,*
him picking J.W. Milam out . . . All Willie
ever uttered, when pressed: *Emmet*
was fourteen . . . I couldn't have walked away.

They whisked Reed off at night to Chicago;
the jury took little more than an hour
to acquit. He married, worked as an orderly,
tried to wear away those memories, but
his widow says he'd often be moaning
in his sleep—still carrying that weight.

And what have we gleaned, sixty years on—
Milam's gang gone, un-convicted, to their maker?
How do we, who commemorate Evers and King
and Birmingham, reckon the escalating tally
of unarmed black men and boys, gunned down
by cops and armed civilians? Will we find
our way to testify—to act, on all that
we've witnessed—or walk away?

Rebecca

Rebecca, known by the surnames
Michael, Martin & Joseph (1807–1851)

You know how the sea whispers
its secrets, when you sit
by the shore? How it inhales
the power of receding surf,
then—a tumbling breath of sand,
shell, stone—in one wave, a truth
revealed. Here's mine: the only
name I'll ever claim in Edgartown
is trouble . . . in and out of jail from age
eleven for non-payment, assault. My own
kin turned me in. I did marry, one year
after William's birth, one Mr. Francis
who'd been jailed *for safekeeping*,
so he would not jump ship again . . . it's
how he landed here. A wonder my death,
the death *of one colored woman, Rebecca*
was noted at all. If I'm remembered,
it will be by tether of birth: my conjuring
mother's wrath to mariners, my son
the whaling master, still at sea when
my five decades of misery washed me up
on shore. I've named myself sorrow.

Sarah, Siren

Sarah Brown Martin, 1832–1911
Dearest Sister Thou hast left us.
—Gravestone, Chappaquidick Island, MA

Bless this sea, the bluff where we
are buried together, this island
on which the Wampanoag grew
corn and potatoes, tended all . . .
Curse the scorn, the fear
that kept us: African, Indian people
all the earth-hued, clustered
on this plantation, at Acquinnah—
all the remote places. On this land
we married. From this island
my beloved William sailed, whaling
master, earned their begrudging
honor. I will only always be known
for making fine soap, and as that Indian
woman who married the Vineyard's only
black whaling captain. His great-grandmother
"Beck" from Guinea found solace too
with an Indian man Elisha Amos,
who left her hay & livestock, the land
her owners would claim. Our history
is buried here, where we farmed and learned
to honor the sea's power. In the end,
we turned our backs, even our gravestone,
against it all. Yet unlike Lot's wife
we move—our melodies stir the oaks,
and in the wind-sculpted yew branches
our spirits sing. They still sing.

Terce: February

There must be a sutra that fits
this mess: lumps of melting snow—
markers of impermanence.
Once the unspoiled beauty
of fields of cotton, ski-slope,
starlit sky—now shoveled and
ploughed, siphoned inward
by sun and gravity. Old snow
with all the elegance of gun-metal
helicopter blades churning overhead.
Soot-smudge tattoos on berms of it,
foot-stomped reminders
of imperfection, dirty laundry.

Only listen for hymn-licks
in the slap of slush from tires,
birdsong layered in like a gospel round.
Then join in, scanning twigs
of gray-barked trees for bud sprits—
that first portent of spring.

Corinthian Baptist, First Sunday

If I silence them, even the stones will shout out.
—Luke 19:39

That palpable hope—a hawk ready
to ride a wind current out over the edge—
lifts the familiar hymns a decibel
higher than the lyrics and organ notes

combined. *Something I never thought*
I'd live to see, the pastor quips, lacing
the air with expectation. Yet he stops;
and the faithful wait for anyone to name

what everyone's on the verge of—yet
all refrain, fearing it will shatter, or
ignite, as a match would in the kitchen
of a house full of dreams. Still, all

the jumpin' chords of gospel bounce
into the autumn morning, as if it *needs*
brightening, scoring the long slow burn
of pent-up desire, pitch rising in each vamp

between verses—until the nodding heads,
hats, eyes seem to signify: this time *even*
the stones will shout out—if need be
in three-part harmony, to pave the way.

Among the Martyrs

Jimmy Lee Jackson was 26, on February 18th,
1965, when a state trooper slammed him
against the cigarette machine in a dark café
where he and other voting rights marchers
sought refuge. Where exactly was I, that night,
three days past my thirteenth birthday,
when the streetlights went out in Marion, Alabama?
Perhaps I was engrossed in history homework,
or dreaming of stealing a kiss with Peter, backstage
after the school play, when Trooper Fowler fired
the fatal shots making Jimmie Lee a martyr
on the road to Selma?
                              Jimmie Lee Jackson was not
among the martyrs, or history, we were studying
in our classrooms full of white girls, daughters
of working-class Catholics, well protected
in our corner of Wilmington, while black citizens
and clergy from city churches set out to join
the Selma campaign. Ms. Lillian, one of these "saints,"
would later teach me a chapter of Delaware history
I'd missed: how the National Guard patrolled
her streets in '68, so we could get to school,
our fathers to work, and our suburbs rest in peace.
Half a century later, an obituary: one James Bonard
Fowler—Jimmie Lee's executioner, stirs up
these histories. I see the ex-trooper finally served
a measly six-month sentence in 2010, after
he sought out a reporter to claim he killed
the unarmed marcher in self-defense. In his story
I trace the contrails of white rage—careering
from workplace assault to Vietnam valor to heroin
trafficking, for which he served more time

than for killing Jimmie Lee. You'd think by now—
after Charleston and Ferguson, after the litanies
of named victims: Trayvon and Michael, Freddie
and Tamir—we would have cornered this hate
like you'd stalk a mountain lion menacing the city.
When will we hear *Who is my neighbor?*
for real, unmask the parallel lives we've led
and re-write these histories, starting
with *why*—and *why not?*

Beyond Doubt

"Truth!" said Pilate. "What does that mean?"
—John 18:38

The minute the preacher named it, I knew:
Thomas was a hero, not the foil. It took guts
for him to offer his hand to Jesus' slit
side, to poke his fingers into the nail holes.
And besides, he was the honest one: *What
do you mean, you saw him?* Logical to ask
his brothers still cowering behind locked
doors. And how come Mary Magdalen
never earns a Sunday solo—her moment
of truth, recognition, in the Easter garden,
her witness buried like the lost coin,
in the mid-week lectionary days after
we celebrate the Resurrection she proclaimed.
In truth, she and Thomas should be our guides:
wail that grief out in some public place,
question, if you doubt, but bloody your hands
in the world's wounds for Christ's sake;
do what it takes to find your way.

Plenty

All those present ate their fill. The fragments remaining,
when gathered up, filled twelve baskets.
—Matthew 14:20

An autumn morning at the farmer's market
just up the road. The sunny roundness of pumpkins
echoes bright orbs of tomatoes among the last truckload
of green-husked sweet corn; eight varieties of apples
cascade from bushel baskets. Sliced samples: stayman,
winesap, empire and jana gold, line up beside
the jugs of fresh pressed cider and cozy rows
of acorn and butternut, zucchini's green fullness.

Far—but not so far—from the dusty roadsides
of Nyeri where we passed farmers
with their plantain and pineapple stacked
on bright blankets, from the muddy market days
of Enugu, where among the traffic and shanties,
vendors hawked bananas piled high in palm baskets,
offered towering bowls of ground cassava
on makeshift tables.

And that farmer we met
in Machakos with three crates of tomatoes balanced
on his rickety bicycle, elated because the new waterpan
irrigates his fields, so he can feed his family and then cart
the surplus to market each week though it takes him
three hours down storm-rutted roads.

The hope
of abundance: plenty of time to ponder seeds and fruit,
water and tools. And to be—like the apostles—amazed
at just how many those five loaves and two fishes feed,
to take measure of the miracle, and all the fragments.

Angels of Korogocho

How are you? How are you? they call out in rapid-fire bursts
of greeting to strangers. They are everywhere, these dusty
angels, their wide-eyes peering from under wool hats,

playing with sticks and all manner of plastic throwaways,
hanging onto the fenders of matatus, clambering onto anything
that's moving through. Korogocho. Same blue sky,

same "blue belly of God" as the Maasai say, but beneath
it on these streets of mud, streets of rubbish and open sewers
three hundred thousand souls make do, selling bananas

and avocado and pineapple; a thousand shillings rents
a tin shack with a leaky roof. Darting among skinny goats
and chickens that feed on maize husks and trash: the children.

Fr. Daniel greets us: *Have you seen my angels?* Their lungs must
be full of tarnished air, with a dump rising like Kilimanjaro
along the edge of the slum. Yet boys in school uniforms appear,

their trousers' neat creases a wonder with no electricity
in sight. Korogocho means chaos, and the fruits of it—small girls
in the odd satin dress or colorful silk scarf—signal a regime

more insidious. It will undermine the aid workers' plan
to re-order this architecture of neglect into some scheme
of sanitary compliance. Meanwhile, the angels line up

raising the palms of their small hands to the visitors:
How are you? How are you?—a gauntlet, each touch
a grimy benediction, dissolving in the rear view.

Nones: Manna in the Desert

The drive out—thirteen miles of one-lane
dirt road, rivers of cloud-shadow wash the feet
of sheer red rock mesas—desolate but
not enough to deter my pilgrimage. Christ
in the Desert, so remote that the vistas
around each hairpin suggest I'm about to drive
off the end of the earth. Luminous clouds float
at eye level in liquid blue at the vanishing point.
My heart sinks as each milepost marker
thwarts my intention: to join the monks
at midday prayer.
                    I could sure use
the balm of plainchant. The green
Rio Chama rages below, hordes
of rafters converge under the distant indigo
shadow of O'Keeffe's tabletop mesa. Add
the occasional specter: a vehicle coming
the other way—breathtaking in extremis.
The hour of Sext has passed, when I enter
the monastery gates, trudge up the dusty path . . .
to the sound of bells! Perhaps I have not missed
the divine office. But as I enter the chapel,
a white-haired monk is escorting guests out.
His cowled brethren bow, and withdraw
behind the icon screen.
                    May I help you?
he asks, as I'm clearly lost.
I'm looking for a quiet place to pray.
His reply: *Will you stay for dinner?*
Stunned, I ask: *when? Now.*
A slight smile. *We'll set another place.*

His welcome, with an inkling
of distant plainchant—why not accept?

An African monk and an Asian novice
pass by each place with serving bowls heaped
with the hearty fruits of garden and farm:
sausage, potatoes and beans, fresh bread
with churned butter—in silence, delicious
as the purple hibiscus garnishing the adobe
walls. *Gaudeamus!* Give thanks. In time
the cook in his white apron brings fruit
for dessert, his handsome Mestizo
features radiate the pleasure he takes
in each silent acknowledgment. We guests
taste the care of planting in each bite,
listen to the lector's measured cadences
reading a pilgrim's account of El Camino
de Santiago de Compostela. As the monks
return to offer seconds, I digest
the medley of their ages and origins. Yet
they each found their way here to pray,
harvest hops and brew ale, make pottery
and music, and when we gather at the 9th hour
before the great window framing sandstone cliffs
behind the altar where stained glass might be,
their voices soar out over the jagged
rocks—join with ravens and raptors
to exalt in the late day light.

Gîte

—shelter, lodging, as for the pilgrims following
the Camino de Santiago de Compostela. Welcome,
gratuitous as the fresh-picked fruit and vegetables,
rounds of cheese in baskets set out by neighbors
here on Rue Peyrin, Auvillar, this morning . . .
and for centuries, before the Garonne River slowed
to the new tune of nuclear plants upstream.
I wonder about today's pilgrims, overtaking me
on the steep hill with their walking sticks and coquilles,
flushed and sweating beneath their backpacks.
What remorse or penance are they carrying,
what resolve launched them toward Finisterre?
Perhaps they are wearing away some grief, or seeking
peace in these vexing days of earthquake, floods
and random violence, now find themselves welcomed
by strangers, entire villages along the Chemin.
Unlike the scenes of barricades at nearly every border
in Europe, calls for walls on our own frontiers. Enough
tear-streaked faces of Muslim women behind barriers
on Lesbos, children holding scrawled pleas for mercy
when the Pope and Patriarch arrive with cameras
that capture the scene, these faces. Images blown
like old newspapers against the chain link fence
of indifference. Those same mothers and children
still wait for welcome. Tent cities pile up at Piraeus,
on Macedonian and Turkish soil, where families
who fled the rubble of Aleppo wait, and children
traumatized by ISIS in Iraqi towns are held in pens
where cattle would be more welcome.
                                    What if
we found it in our hearts to empty our bulging pantries
and deploy an army of welcome to greet these pilgrims?

Then perhaps young Adam, who escaped the mudbricks
of Darfur cotton fields to cross Egypt, cast his lot
in a flimsy boat that washed up on Italy's boot heel,
would not be huddled with Ethiopian migrants,
Gambians and Somalis in a makeshift campground
beside Lake Como's glitter. No gîte or asylum here,
no baskets of fresh fruit and cheese. Instead,
we arm the Swiss border with night goggles
and drones to hunt them down, rather than
offering to oil their foreheads and feet, as if
welcoming honored guests. Or like pilgrims
climbing the next stage of the Way—
their own steep ascent.

Revisiting the Parable of the Sower on Martha's Vineyard

So was it the seeds
scattered in sandy soil,
or the sea-salted rain
that bred this gaudy display—
fuchsia and blue-violet hydrangea
on this wind-kissed day?
A catbird teases me
toward my own rock-clotted
acreage. Shoots of faith
thick with thistle, return
each season. Some looming
loss bids me sift anew.

Today, the broken glass
of cruelty, indifference.
An ice shelf the size
of Delaware calves
into the Southern Ocean,
as millions launch out
into perilous seas, toward
all our barricades and lack
of faith. Still each day
the sower's hand offers
some momentary grace: wind
in the mainsail, that osprey's cry,
our grandson's shriek of joy,
to water what's sown.

Vigil, Day Three

> *Evening came . . . and morning followed, the third day.*
> —Genesis 1:12

It's the tiny things that break the silence,
break your heart—moments you stand
helpless against the rip tide of a diagnosis,
regimen of treatment, the mortal undertow
none of us will manage to break from.
The slow drip of water in the IV, each drop
perhaps a tiny savior. The soft chime
of a wooden popsicle stick dropped
into an empty water glass, brings
a sigh of relief, a slight hope. Perhaps
the orange ice we offered, still visible
in tinted lips might slake his hunger,
allay a measure of thirst. Meanwhile,
we mark time moving mattresses, install
a sick bed, find one weight we can carry.

Mi-Carême

I.

Dust to dust—my father's last gulp of Communion wine
this time last year. Pastor Rebecca tells of witnessing her first
cremation: "It was like a garage. So bare." No cross or censer,
no way to temper the brute force of flame.

Ash Wednesday,
a crowd of seagulls ascends from a garbage-strewn street,
a cloud of swallows forms, disperses, re-forms above me
as if resisting the penitential in their soaring.
Nubs of hyacinth break the garden's crust with bud.

II.

New Orleans in the aftermath of another Mardi Gras.
Disconcerting, the detritus: live oak draped with shiny beads,
abandoned port-o-potties, with the ghosts of desperate refugees
still inhabiting the I-10 overpass.

Weather beaten
shotgun shacks between the purple, green and gold
buntinged balconies, punctuate this inversion:
the more intense the sorrow, the more exuberance.
It's *in the shadow* of the valley of death, we dance—

this Second Line.

III.

March arrives with the anniversaries of family deaths
piled like sticks of dry tinder. I listen to our friend's young
widow reckoning the sudden crash of absence—

                                        I reckon
Laetare's command summons us not just
to pause from The Fast—allowing flowers, weddings
and loaves for relief—but also to embrace
the inextricable: rose and violet strands entwined.

Vespers, Hunting Creek

After storms, after days of rain
        a shallow creek at nightfall—
the scent of honeysuckle drifts
        from shore, as we anchor
under a sudden canopy of stars

the halfmoon's reflected
        in a pool of light, floating iris
        winking eye of night
centered among
        a Rorschach of trees
leaking their likenesses
        into the waters

around us, strokes
of the invisible—fish rippling
        the dark of our memories:
friends passing swiftly from us,
        our own numbered days

sinful, it seems
        to disturb this stillness
with word. Still the longing:
        Nunc Dimittis,
        Into your hands . . . Salva nos.

Let nightfall
        honor them
with its silence, pray
        only the psalm of osprey
        and tree frogs
commingling
        with stars.

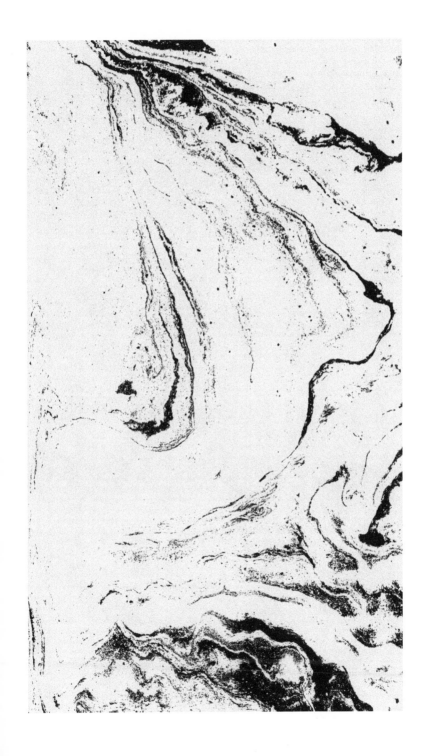

NOTES TO THE POEMS

Illumination
In 1995, St. John's Abbey, Collegeville, Minnesota, commissioned
Donald Jackson, "The Queen's Calligrapher," to produce the first
illuminated Bible in over 500 years. It was completed in 2007.

Riff
The particulars of geology and ecology, wildlife, flora and fauna of
the Sierra mountain region that inspired this poem, I owe to David
Lucas, naturalist, whose guided walks for the poets of the *Community
of Writers* have stocked a storehouse of imagery and scientific detail
that also appears in "Mindful," "From Birdsong," "Roots, Exposed,"
and "At the First Canonical Hour."

Walking the Elements, Beara Peninsula
During five days of silence and meditation practice at Anam Cara
Writers Retreat in County Cork, Ireland, this poem took shape.
The *Silent, Guided Elements Retreat,* led by poet and reiki master Kim
Richardson, invited participants to connect our breath (or energy—
the "ch'i" referenced in section II) to the elements of earth, water, fire,
and air we experienced in the stunning Beara landscape.

Heist
This poem, written during a residency at Virginia Center for
the Creative Arts, takes part of its inspiration from the work of
other resident artists, in particular the light sculptures of Florence
Carbonne and the musical compositions of Caroline Keys.

At the First Canonical Hour, Lauds, Terce: February, Nones: Manna in the Desert,
and *Vespers, Hunting Creek*
The anchor poems in the final section refer to the hours at which
monastic prayers are traditionally said. These poems are part of a

longer sequence and were included in a chapbook, *Waking Hours*, published in 2017 by the Franciscan University of Steubenville, Ohio, in their annual chapbook series.

Bop: The Truth and Nothing But
The Bop form was invented by Aafa Michael Weaver. The quote in the refrain comes from Adrienne Rich, in the title essay of her collection *Arts of the Possible*, first given as the Troy Lecture, University of Massachusetts, 1997. "Every real poem is the breaking of an existing silence, and the first question we might ask any poem is, *What kind of voice is breaking silence, and what kind of silence is being broken?*"

Witness, Among the Martyrs
For many of the details of Willie Reed's life, I am in debt to an obituary and remembrance in the *Washington Post* written by Emily Langer in July 2013. Similarly, an obituary of James Bonard Fowler, written by Adam Bernstein, also in the *Washington Post*, in July, 2015.

Sarah, Siren and *Rebecca*
The voices of these two women came to me during a residency at the Martha's Vineyard Writers and Artists Retreat. I am grateful to the research and historical markers of the African American History Trail of Martha's Vineyard for their inspiration.

ACKNOWLEDGMENTS

I am grateful to the following publications in which versions of these poems have appeared.

Antiphon	Riff: What it Takes
Assisi	On the Feast of St. Francis, Parable, Revisiting the Parable of the Sower on Martha's Vineyard
Atlanta Review	Waking Heaney in Edgartown, MA
Blueline	This Far
Broadkill Review	Their voices
Christian Century	Beyond Doubt, Terce
Comstock Review	Sarah, Siren
Connecticut River Review	Rebecca
Cresset	Lauds, Aberdeen Creek
Delaware Review	Half Italian
Hidden Channel Zine	Museum of Divine Statues
Hunger Mountain	Medium, Starlings
Little Patuxent Review	Mindful, and Vespers, Hunting Creek
Modern Haiku	The Gleaners
Northern Virginia Review	Heist
Notre Dame Review	Mi-Carême
Poetry East	Lumen de Lumine, Reliquary, Plenty
Potomac Review	Sustenance, Twilight Ardgroom
Presence	Vigil, Day Three
Rockhurst Review	At the First Canonical Hour
Sligo Review	Gîte
Smartish Pace	Roots, Exposed, and Terrestrial
Spiritus	Teresa, Crossing Over
Split This Rock	Halim, Waiting
Vox Populi	Among the Martyrs, Half-Italian, Mindful, Witness

In addition, "Bop: The Truth and Nothing But" and "Mindful" were included in *Adrienne Rich: A Tribute Anthology*, published by Split Oak Press. "At the Mariner's Chapel" was featured (Third Prize) in the *Image/New York Encounter Poetry Contest*, 2017. "The Gleaners" also appeared in *Nothing in the Window*, the 2012 Red Moon Anthology of English-language haiku.

The poems "Their Voices," "Requiem at Compline," "Corinthian Baptist, First Sunday," and "Plenty" also appeared in *In the Margins* (Cincinnati, OH: Cherry Grove Collections, 2017).

ABOUT PARACLETE PRESS

Who We Are

As the publishing arm of the Community of Jesus, Paraclete Press presents a full expression of Christian belief and practice—from Catholic to Evangelical, from Protestant to Orthodox, reflecting the ecumenical charism of the Community and its dedication to sacred music, the fine arts, and the written word. We publish books, recordings, sheet music, and video/DVDs that nourish the vibrant life of the church and its people.

What We Are Doing

BOOKS

PARACLETE PRESS BOOKS show the richness and depth of what it means to be Christian. While Benedictine spirituality is at the heart of who we are and all that we do, our books reflect the Christian experience across many cultures, time periods, and houses of worship.
We have many series, including *Paraclete Essentials; Paraclete Fiction; Paraclete Poetry; Paraclete Giants;* and for children and adults, *All God's Creatures,* books about animals and faith; and *San Damiano Books,* focusing on Franciscan spirituality. Others include *Voices from the Monastery* (men and women monastics writing about living a spiritual life today), *Active Prayer,* and new for young readers: *The Pope's Cat.* We also specialize in gift books for children on the occasions of Baptism and First Communion, as well as other important times in a child's life, and books that bring creativity and liveliness to any adult spiritual life.
The MOUNT TABOR BOOKS series focuses on the arts and literature as well as liturgical worship and spirituality; it was created in conjunction with the Mount Tabor Ecumenical Centre for Art and Spirituality in Barga, Italy.

MUSIC

The PARACLETE RECORDINGS label represents the internationally acclaimed choir *Gloriæ Dei Cantores*, the *Gloriæ Dei Cantores Schola*, and the other instrumental artists of the *Arts Empowering Life Foundation*. Paraclete Press is the exclusive North American distributor for the Gregorian chant recordings from St. Peter's Abbey in Solesmes, France. Paraclete also carries all of the Solesmes chant publications for Mass and the Divine Office, as well as their academic research publications.

In addition, PARACLETE PRESS SHEET MUSIC publishes the work of today's finest composers of sacred choral music, annually reviewing over 1,000 works and releasing between 40 and 60 works for both choir and organ.

VIDEO

Our video/DVDs offer spiritual help, healing, and biblical guidance for a broad range of life issues including grief and loss, marriage, forgiveness, facing death, understanding suicide, bullying, addictions, Alzheimer's, and Christian formation.

Learn more about us at our website
www.paracletepress.com
or phone us toll-free at 1.800.451.5006

SCAN
TO
READ
MORE

YOU MAY ALSO BE INTERESTED IN . . .

ALMOST ENTIRELY
Jennifer Wallace
ISBN 978-1-61261-859-3 | $18

"Put together in a way that makes you want to get to the end of the poem and see just what this author is up to. Compelling." —*America*

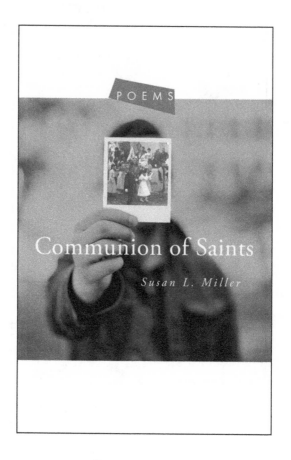

POEMS

Communion of Saints

Susan L. Miller

COMMUNION OF SAINTS
Susan L. Miller
ISBN 978-1-61261-858-6 | $18

"An energetic, almost ecstatic, new mode of reinvigorating an-
cient modes of faith." —*Presence*

DREAMING OF STONES

Poems

CHRISTINE VALTERS PAINTNER

DREAMING OF STONES
Christine Valters Paintner
ISBN 978-1-64060-108-6 | $18

"The flash of light, the kernel of truth that goes deeper
and more mystically into the heart of the universe
than fact and faith can hope to do."
—Joan Chittister, OSB

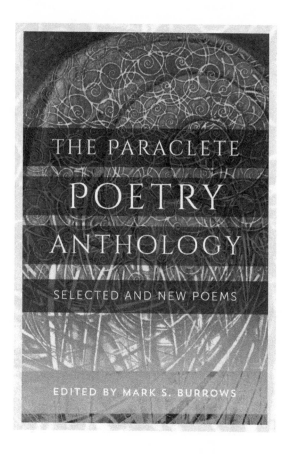

THE PARACLETE POETRY ANTHOLOGY
SELECTED AND NEW POEMS
edited by Mark S. Burrows
ISBN 978-1-61261-906-4 | $20

"Altogether, the range of poetic expression here encompasses
spiritual journaling, prayer, legends and biography,
visionary and ordinary mysticism, nature-contemplation,
and, of course, prayer, as well as formally relaxed and
precise individual poems. A worthy showcase."
—*BOOKLIST*

CPSIA information can be obtained
at www.ICGtesting.com
Printed in the USA
FSHW011252040820
72695FS

9 781640 602625